ROUGH & READY
RAILROADERS

A. S. GINTZLER

FITZGERALD BOOKS

BETHANY, MISSOURI

Acknowledgments

To the railroaders and their chroniclers.

First Hardcover Library Bound Edition
Published in 1998 by Fitzgerald Books
P.O. Box 505, Bethany, Missouri 64424

Library of Congress Cataloging-in-Publication Data
Gintzler, A. S.
Rough and Ready railroaders / A. S. Gintzler
  p.   cm.
  Includes index.
ISBN 1-887238-12-3
1. Railroads—United States—Juvenile literature. [1. Railroads—History.] I. Title.
TF23.G56 1998
385'.0973—dc20   97-78366
                                                  CIP
                                                  AC

Logo & Cover Design: Paul Perlow
Interior Design and Typography: Linda Braun
Illustrations: Chris Brigman
Printer: Burton & Mayer, Inc.
Title page photo: Railroad workers
    © Denver Public Library
    Western History Department

Construction crew with a woodburning locomotive, 1885

The Bettmann Archive

CONTENTS

The First Railroads

The first steam locomotives came smoking out of England in the 1820s. The locomotive, or "Iron Horse," quickly entered history in a rush of snorting smoke and led the world into a "machine age." Older methods of transportation were soon to be left behind in the dust.

In the early 1800s, the United States was a new country with lots of land. Most people lived in the eastern part of the country, and pioneers were just beginning to explore the western frontier. When people traveled, they walked, rode horses, or traveled in stagecoaches and horse-drawn wagons. Most heavy loads were sent by boat on rivers or canals.

Early U.S. rail cars were pulled along tracks by horses. In Boston, horses pulled wagons on wooden rails. Horse-drawn trains also hauled coal from Pennsylvania's mines. But Americans doubted that railroads could ever be used to transport people or freight over long distances.

The Bettmann Archive

Puffing Billy, *an early locomotive*

HOW STEAM LOCOMOTIVES WORK

When water is boiled in a kettle, it expands into a gas called steam. Old-time locomotives were basically steam factories on wheels. Wood or coal was burned in a firebox to heat water in a boiler. The steam from the boiling water pressed against a cylinder in a tube called a piston. When the pistons slid in the cylinder, they pushed rods that were attached to the engine's driving wheels, and that made the locomotive move. Trains carried water for producing steam in the fuel car, called a tender car, directly behind the engine.

Filling up at the water tank

Bystanders scoffed when a young mechanical engineer named Horatio Allen fired up the *Stourbridge Lion* in Pennsylvania. His English-made steam engine, with its wheels connected by long rods, looked like a giant mechanical grasshopper. But Allen drove the *Lion* safely over six miles of track for the first locomotive ride in the United States.

The Tom Thumb *locomotive races a horse-drawn wagon*

Even the builders of the horse-drawn Baltimore & Ohio railroad doubted the usefulness of steam locomotives. The B & O was formed in 1827 to connect Baltimore to the Ohio River. Tracks were carved from wood with flat iron rails strapped to the top. On August 28, 1830, a small American-built locomotive called *Tom Thumb* was challenged to a race across B & O track. The horse-drawn challenger won when an engine belt slipped on the locomotive.

Nevertheless, B & O officials were impressed by *Tom Thumb*'s overall performance. In 1831, the American engine *York* sped along B & O tracks at 35 miles an hour. Steam locomotion was catching on.

Horatio Allen convinced builders of a new railroad in South Carolina to try steam instead of horses. In 1831, Allen's new engine, the six-horsepower *Best Friend of Charleston*, became the first American locomotive in regular service. It hauled railroad building supplies and west-bound passengers at 21 miles an hour. By 1835, nearly 16,000 passengers a year were riding South Carolina's Charleston & Hamburg railroad.

Americans were discovering that locomotives were cheaper and faster than other means of transportation. Businessmen and investors turned from building canals to constructing railroads. By 1840, there were 5,000 miles of railroad track in the U.S. Some 200 railroad lines were in operation or being planned. Soon, every town wanted a railroad running through it, bringing people and trade. America had entered the railroad age.

Working on the Railroad

In the 1860s, railroaders began laying tracks that would stretch across the United States from Boston to San Francisco. Before this transcontinental railroad was completed, cross-country travel took many months by wagon or ocean voyage. Coast-to-coast travel by railroad shortened the trip to about a week.

Railroad workers labored almost four years to complete the first cross-country railway. They covered 1,800 miles of wilderness with iron tracks. It was back-breaking, dangerous work. Most of the workers were immigrants who had come to America from China and Ireland. Others were freed slaves and men who had fought in the Civil War.

Each worker belonged to a crew, and each crew had its own job. Surveyors explored the land ahead of the building crews. They decided which parts of the countryside would be easiest to build through, and made maps for the builders to follow. Locomotives could not pull heavy loads straight up hills, so the surveyors mapped routes through level valleys and marked paths that zigzagged up steep inclines. Tunnels were built to make passage through the mountains possible.

The grading crew's job was to make a sturdy roadbed on which to build tracks. A roadbed is a foundation of crushed rock. The grading crew evened out the bumps and dips in the ground to make it level. On the Union Pacific line, which crossed the Great Plains, graders could make 100 miles of roadbed ready in a month. Work slowed down, however, when graders had to build wooden bridges across rivers or blast through mountains of solid rock. Building tunnels through mountains was very risky work. First, steel drivers pounded drills into the rock to make blasting holes. These deep holes were then filled with black blasting powder and ignited. Many workers were killed by flying stones when tunnels were blasted out of the Sierra Nevada mountains in California.

The Bettmann Archive

A scraper preparing roadbed for the Northern Pacific railroad

Workers laying rails on the Central Pacific line

After the grading crews came the tracklayers, who put down ties on the roadbed. Ties are wooden beams placed one after another with the same amount of space between each one, like steps on a ladder. They support the rails on which trains run.

It took four strong men to lay a rail on top of the ties. Each rail was thirty feet long and weighed 600 pounds. Rail handlers put two rails in place every minute.

A piece of iron called a "fishplate" was used to bolt the ends of the rails together and keep them straight. Spikes kept the rails connected to the wooden ties.

Finally, workers had to be sure that the two rails were exactly the same distance apart so that the train's wheels would sit directly on top of them. The distance between the rails was called the gauge. It wasn't until 1886 that all tracks were built to a standard gauge of 4 feet 8½ inches. This allowed locomotives from one railroad to run on the tracks of any other railroad.

WORK TRAINS

As soon as one section of track was finished, work trains took supplies to the builders at the end of the line. These trains pulled up to 12 cars filled with rails, spikes, tools, and food. Some even had blacksmith shops and bunks for sleeping. When the crews had all the supplies they needed, they could build one to two miles of track each day.

Crews slept in bunkhouses pulled along the tracks

Better Trains and More Track

Since railroads were such a new invention, builders didn't have many rules to follow when laying down tracks. They had to learn from their mistakes.

The Baltimore & Ohio first tried using ties made of stone, but found that wooden ties made trains ride more smoothly. Wooden ties, however, rotted into the ground after being exposed to months of harsh weather. Eventually, railroad builders found that soaking the ties in oil and chemical preservatives helped keep the wooden ties from rotting.

When it rained, though, tracks and ties sank into the muddy ground. Builders solved the mud problem by building a roadbed to support the ties and rails. The crushed rock of the roadbed drained rainwater away from the tracks.

Rails changed, too, as the railroads grew. The first rails were made of wood with flat iron bands strapped to the top. But often the weight of a train would loosen an iron band, making the end of it curl up and slice through the floor of a train car.

Passengers were sometimes injured or killed by these rails, which trainmen called "snakeheads," until solid iron rails were invented. By the 1860s, stronger steel rails replaced the iron ones. Train wheels had rims called flanges that kept the cars from slipping off the rails.

The first passenger cars were stagecoaches attached to train car wheels

At first, train passengers rode in stagecoaches attached to train wheels, or in boxcars, or even on train car roofs. In 1837, a train line in Pennsylvania designed large eight-wheeled passenger coaches. Later, sleeping cars with beds and sinks were built so passengers could rest comfortably on long overnight rides.

By the 1840s, locomotives were speeding along tracks at 60 miles an hour, pulling as many as thirty cars. Train crews had to find ways to signal each other, so that trains on the same track wouldn't crash head on. One train had to be signaled to pull off the main track onto a side track to let the other pass.

NEW AND IMPROVED LOCOMOTIVES

American locomotive builders were always working to improve their steam engines. V-shaped frames called "cow catchers" were attached to the front of engines to keep the tracks clear. A special smokestack over the furnace kept chunks of burning wood from flying out and hurting passengers. Headlights were added for night travel and steam whistles for signaling.

A fully equipped locomotive

Train crews learned to use whistles, signal poles, flags, and lanterns to communicate between stations. By the 1850s, electric telegraph signals were being used to direct train traffic.

By 1854, it seemed possible to build a transcontinental railroad, a route that would stretch from coast to coast. Railroaders, merchants, and settlers began to talk about how it could be done. But politicians disagreed over whether the tracks should cross the southern or northern part of the country.

President Abraham Lincoln and Congress knew that a cross-country railroad would help connect the new western states to the eastern United States. So in 1862 they passed the Pacific Railroad Act. This act promised to pay the railroads in money and land for each mile of cross-country track they built.

Two companies were formed to build the cross-country railroad. The Central Pacific would build from Sacramento east, while the Union Pacific would build from Omaha west. But before work started, the Civil War broke out.

Flagmen waved flags to signal to the engineer

Trains in the Civil War

The debate over a railroad route west ended in 1861 when 11 Southern states seceded from the Union—they formed their own government and said they were no longer part of the United States. The Civil War had begun.

At that time there were 31,246 miles of railroad track in the U.S., but only 10,000 of those miles were in the South. The northern states, called the Union, had more industry and railroads, while the southern states, called the Confederacy, had mostly farmland and used mainly riverboats for transportation.

The Civil War was the world's first railroad war. Both armies used trains to bring troops and supplies far into enemy territory. In 1862, the Union Army formed the U.S. Military Railway—the letters USMR appeared on all Union trains. Hospital trains were also used during the Civil War. Military and medical trains had right-of-way on all rail lines so that troops and supplies could be moved as quickly as possible.

The Bettmann Archive

Union soldiers gathered around their cannon

Since the Union had more railroads, it was able to move many soldiers quickly, and this helped win battles. The Union army had four lines running east to west through the North, but the South had just two east-west lines. Both Southern lines were open to attack either by Union armies invading over land, or by the Union navy attacking along the coast.

SHERMAN'S MARCH ALONG THE TRACKS

In the final days of the Civil War, Union General William Sherman marched to Atlanta, Georgia, with 100,000 soldiers. During the 200-day march through the South, Sherman's forces were supplied by the railroad. Sixteen trains left Nashville each day with 200,000 pounds of supplies on each train. Sherman's Atlanta campaign and defeat of the South would not have been possible without the railroad.

The Bettmann Archive

General William Sherman

Fierce battles raged at Nashville, Tennessee, the center of the South's rail system. By 1862, Union troops had captured Nashville as the command post for the U.S. Military Railroad. More than 200 Union locomotives and 3,000 cars operated out of Nashville over 1,200 miles of track.

Meanwhile, the Union's Baltimore & Ohio (B & O) line was attacked by Confederate armies. Troops led by General Stonewall Jackson captured a fleet of B & O engines in Virginia and transported them south.

The Louisville & Nashville (L & N) line running between Kentucky and Tennessee tried to stay out of the war. Like the state of Kentucky, the L & N didn't choose sides. Still, Union and Confederate armies fought for control of the line and kept L & N crews busy repairing wrecked track.

A locomotive wrecked by Union soldiers, 1865

The Bettmann Archive

The Bettmann Archive

A USMR train crossing a trestle

To stop the enemy, soldiers of both armies became skilled railroad destroyers. Union armies had a tool that looked like an iron claw, which they used to tear up and twist track. Confederate raiders in Missouri tore up rails, burned ties, and wrecked trains on the Hannibal and St. Joe line. Rails were heated over burning ties, then twisted while red-hot.

Both armies tried to stop the enemy by ruining their railroads. In the end, it worked. The Union Army won the war by destroying the South's railways.

Blasting Through the Sierras

While soldiers were still fighting the Civil War in the East, the Central Pacific began building a new railroad in the West. In January 1863 two of the owners of the Central Pacific led ground-breaking ceremonies at Sacramento, California, for the railroad they hoped would cross the country.

Central Pacific track would run east from Sacramento and climb 7,000 feet into the Sierra Nevada mountains before going down again into the Nevada desert. From the start, the work went slowly.

Building supplies were hard to get, because the armies back East were using wood and steel to rebuild tracks destroyed in Civil War battles. Also, rails, spikes, and construction trains had to be shipped by boat from the eastern U.S. around the tip of South America—a 17,000-mile journey that took six months.

The first shipment of supplies didn't arrive until October 1863. On board was the first locomotive to reach California, the *Governor Stanford*. While being unloaded, the 65,000-pound engine was almost dumped overboard into the sea.

Work crews blasting a path through the mountains

SIERRA SNOW SHEDS

During the harsh winter of 1867-68, Central Pacific crews built track down the eastern slope of the Sierras. Three locomotives, 40 cars, and 40 miles of track material were hauled on giant sleds over deep snow. To keep roadbeds clear for construction and travel, snow shed tunnels were built. The wooden sheds protected 37 miles of roadbed from avalanches, falling snow, and 80-foot drifts. It took 2,500 workers, 65 million feet of timber, and five months just to build the sheds.

Snow sheds kept the tracks clear

By February 1864, only 18 miles of track had been laid east of Sacramento. But the Central Pacific was already carrying passengers on that line from Sacramento to the Junction station at Roseville. Four months later, the rails had reached the Sierra Nevadas, a mountain range of solid granite. An army of workers would be needed to blast and tunnel through 6,213 feet of rock.

The Central Pacific hired Chinese immigrants to become railroad workers. The Chinese worked for lower wages than other crews, and they were more orderly and reliable. By the time the Civil War ended in 1865, 7,000 Chinese men were building the railroad on the western slope of the Sierras.

Chinese crews working near Sacramento, California

Chinese crews ate dried oysters and fish, dried fruit and mushrooms, bamboo shoots, rice, and vegetables. Their diet was more varied than the beef, beans, bread, and potatoes the white crews ate.

By November 1866, Central Pacific track covered 94 miles and climbed 6,000 feet to Cisco on the western slope of the Sierras. Chinese crews then began drilling and blasting a system of 15 tunnels through the mountain granite. Crews used 550 kegs of black blasting powder every day, working around the clock in three 8-hour shifts. Sometimes it took all day just to blast through five feet of rock.

The tunnels varied in length, from the 271-foot Emigrant Gap to the 1,650-foot Summit Tunnel. When winter blizzards buried tunnel entrances under tons of snow, crews burrowed through the snow drifts. Work on Summit Tunnel alone took nine months and 8,000 men to complete.

By August 1867, the last of the Sierra tunnels was finished. Crews began laying track down the eastern slope of the Sierras. Tracks reached Reno, Nevada, in June 1868 and crossed the Nevada desert to Utah in 1869. In six years, 700 miles of open country had been covered by Central Pacific track.

Tracks Across the Prairie

The Union Pacific company, which was building tracks across the country from east to west, got off to a slow start. Ground-breaking ceremonies were held at Omaha, Nebraska, in December 1863, but the Civil War and money problems caused delays. When Thomas Durant took control of the Union Pacific, he hired chief engineer Grenville Dodge to supervise construction.

Dodge mapped out a westbound route that followed the old Oregon Trail along Nebraska's Platte River. But the first mile of track wasn't put down until July 1865. By then the Civil War had ended. Former soldiers, including Irish, German, and Scandinavian immigrants, along with freed slaves, were hired on as building crews. Over the next 15 months, crews graded roadbeds and laid track across 250 miles of prairie. By early 1866, about 2,000 workers set up camp at North Platte, Nebraska. As the year ended, tracks reached 300 miles west of Omaha. But supplies were slow to reach construction crews. Rails, ties, and trains were first shipped to Omaha by way of the Missouri River. Then in 1867, supplies began to be shipped by train on the Northwestern line, which stretched across Iowa.

Railroad builders crossing the Great Plains

The Bettmann Archive

West of North Platte, Nebraska, the Union Pacific builders faced the Continental Divide, a series of mountain ranges snaking south from Canada. The Oregon Trail had crossed these Rocky Mountains through South Pass in Wyoming. But Chief Engineer Dodge found a shorter route by accident when his survey team was attacked by Indians fighting the railroad. The crew escaped through an unexplored mountain pass south in Wyoming. This pass through the Rockies became the Union Pacific route across the Divide.

THE BIG TRESTLE

Union Pacific crews began building across a deep gorge on Utah's Promontory mountain in March 1869. Construction engineers designed the bridge, called a trestle, as a temporary structure only. They planned to support it later by filling the gorge with earth. Crews blasted deep cuts in the limestone to support the trestle roadbed. The Big Trestle took more than a month to complete and spanned 400 feet. In May 1869, the U.P.'s engine No. 119 crossed the trestle, 85 feet above the gorge.

The Promontory Gorge trestle

Through 1867, crews worked to cover 245 miles of Indian country with railroad track. By October, the track had reached the new town of Cheyenne. Meanwhile, crews were already building gravel roadbed 400 miles west into Utah.

Work in Wyoming slowed during the winter, but tracklayers crossed the Continental Divide by spring 1868. Union Pacific track climbed 8,242 feet to Sherman Summit before descending the western slope to the plains. Then more than 10,000 men worked across Wyoming's desert, putting down track to Utah.

By the time winter came again, the builders had reached Utah's Wasatch Mountains. The crews worked through blizzards and snow drifts on top of Echo Summit just as the Central Pacific crews had done in the Sierras. To keep men working under such harsh conditions, the Union Pacific owners doubled the workers' wages.

Finally, in March 1869, the rails reached Ogden, Utah. Union Pacific crews had covered more than 1,000 miles of plains, river valleys, and mountains with iron rails.

In order for trains to climb steep hills, mountain tracks were laid in a zigzag pattern

Native Americans and the Railroad

A gathering of Cheyenne chiefs

During the 1600s and 1700s, European settlers conquered Native American peoples in the East and took most of their land. By 1783, pioneers had pushed west to the Mississippi River. Native tribes tried to defend their homelands against the European invaders, but they couldn't stop the westward flow of settlers.

In 1830, Congress passed the Indian Removal Act, which forced eastern tribes to move west of the Mississippi to territories known as "Indian country." But even that wasn't far enough for builders of the transcontinental railroad.

In the 1850s, railroad companies mapped out routes across Indian country, and native tribes were forced to move again. Starting in 1854, the government put up fences to keep the Delaware, Missouri, and Fox tribes off of their lands. Tens of millions of acres were claimed by the government, and the tribes were pushed west into Nebraska and Kansas.

In the 1860s, the railroads began laying track through the Great Plains—the hunting grounds of Cheyenne and Sioux peoples. These high plains were home to huge buffalo herds that supplied the native tribes with meat and hides for clothing and shelter. It was on the Plains that the Indians took their stand against the Iron Horse and the men who built it.

In 1867, Indian war parties attacked workers on the Union Pacific and Kansas Pacific lines. In response, the government sent out soldiers on horses to guard railroad workers. The railroads also tried to starve the Indians out of the region by destroying the huge buffalo herds they depended on for survival.

Native Americans had lived on the Great Plains for thousands of years before the Iron Horse came

14

On August 6, 1867, a band of Cheyenne Indians derailed a railroad car carrying five telegraph workers near Plum Creek, Nebraska. The Indians killed four and wounded one who got away. That same day, the Cheyennes pulled up rails and wrecked a freight train, killing the engineer and fireman.

In Kansas, General George Armstrong Custer led attacks against Indian villages, forcing the tribes to move farther west. On November 27, 1867, Custer attacked a tribe of peaceful Cheyenne led by Chief Black Kettle. This slaughter made the Indians even angrier at the railroad and the army.

The Bettmann Archive

Indians, however, could not succeed against thousands of U.S. soldiers with bigger weapons. As the railroad pushed into Colorado and Wyoming, tribes were forced to move farther west and north.

In California and Nevada, the native Paiute and Shoshone tribes didn't put up a fight against the railroad. Central Pacific officials signed treaties with tribal leaders, allowing them free rides on the railroad. Native crews were also hired to work alongside the Chinese building crews.

Indians couldn't stop the railroad builders

The railroad, together with white settlers' westward migration, drove the Native American tribes off their lands, forcing them onto reservations or destroying them completely. The American Indians' traditional way of life was forever changed in just a few years by the Iron Horse.

SITTING BULL'S WAR

During the 1800s, the Sioux people were driven west again and again by white settlers, miners, and construction of the railroad. By 1870, they had followed the buffalo herds into northern Wyoming and hoped to settle there. But a few years later the Northern Pacific Railroad entered Sioux country. Chief Sitting Bull and his men fought General Custer at the Battle of the Little Bighorn and won. But the railroad went through anyway, and Sitting Bull was forced to flee to Canada.

Race to the Finish

The Pacific Railroad Act had promised that the government would pay the railroads in money and land for each mile of cross-country track they built. It also said that the Central Pacific should build from California toward the east, and the Union Pacific should build from Nebraska toward the west. But it didn't say where the rails would meet.

Both companies rushed to lay more track and collect more in government payments. By 1869, the race from east and west was going full-steam in Utah. Survey crews from both companies mapped out routes that headed toward Utah's Great Salt Lake. But instead of meeting, the two paths passed each other by.

Union Pacific and Central Pacific crews tried to sabotage each other's work

Grading crews from both railroads were now working almost side by side, preparing roadbeds for two different lines of track. Workers did whatever they could to slow the other company down. Union Pacific crews rolled boulders down onto the Central Pacific workers, while Central Pacific crews set off blasts without warning the Union Pacific crews nearby. Workers were hurt and killed before government and railroad officials agreed to join the lines at Promontory, Utah.

May 8, 1869, was the official date set for the meeting and joining of rails. By May 1, tracklayers for both lines had reached Promontory Summit. Promontory became a boom town overnight, filled with hundreds of workers who suddenly had the time and money to drink, gamble, and fight.

Four days later, the Central Pacific's *Jupiter* Engine No. 60 arrived from California decorated with red, white, and blue banners. The officials on board had brought a gold spike, a silver-plated sledge hammer, and a polished wooden tie. But the "golden spike" ceremony scheduled for May 8 had to be postponed when the train carrying Union Pacific officials was delayed. The train had been sidetracked on May 6 by angry Union Pacific construction crews in Wyoming. They refused to let the train pass until the railroad paid their wages. Two days later, the workers were paid $253,000 and the train continued on. The Union Pacific officials arrived in Promontory on May 10.

Reporters, photographers, government officials, and townsfolk gathered around the tracks while one crew from each company laid down the last two rails.

TEN MILES OF TRACK IN A DAY

The Bettmann Archive

Until April 1869, the Union Pacific line held the record for laying down the longest stretch of track in one day—a whopping eight miles. But the construction chief of the Central Pacific made a $10,000 bet that his men could top it. At 7 a.m. on April 28, the crews began building. The men laid about a mile of track an hour. By 7 p.m. they'd put down 10 miles and 56 feet of track. Eight rail handlers that day had lifted 2 million pounds of iron.

A Union Pacific construction train

Telegraph wires had been attached to the last spike so that it would conduct the electric telegraph signal. The tap of the hammer against the spike was supposed to send a telegraph signal to nine American cities.

Leland Stanford of the Central Pacific swung the silver hammer at the spike—and missed. Then Thomas Durant of the Union Pacific took a swing—and missed too. A telegraph operator tapped out a "done" message anyway, while Grenville Dodge, chief engineer of the Union Pacific, hammered the spike into place. The engines pulled forward so their cow catchers were touching. Champagne corks popped. The first transcontinental railroad was complete.

The Bettmann Archive

Celebrating the completion of the transcontinental railroad, May 10, 1869

First Cross-Country Travelers

Transcontinental train service began on May 15, 1869, just five days after the tracks were connected in Utah. But the first trains to cross the country didn't go straight through. Passengers had to change trains several times to reach California.

Travelers from eastern cities like Boston and New York first rode the Michigan Central Railroad to Chicago. There they connected with the Rock Island or Northwestern lines bound for Council Bluffs, Iowa. In Council Bluffs travelers rode stagecoaches from the train depot to the river bank, then took a ferry across the Missouri River to Omaha. Finally, they boarded the Union Pacific train in Omaha for the five- to seven-day trip to California.

Clerks for the Atlantic & Pacific R.R. in front of their office

Travelers rode in simple or fancy passenger cars depending on how much they paid. Tickets on crowded immigrant cars with plain wooden seats and no place to sleep cost $40. For about $120 passengers rode first class in Pullman Palace Cars. George Pullman invented the Palace sleeper cars in the 1860s. They had soft cushioned seats that converted into beds at night. Upper beds folded out of the sides of the car above the seats. Thick green curtains pulled across the beds for privacy.

Inside a crowded sleeping car

Pullman also designed a hotel car that looked like a long hotel lobby and a dining car that could serve 12-course meals. *The Pacific Hotel Express*, complete with dining and hotel cars, made just one run a week during the 1870s.

In the first years of transcontinental train travel, passengers ate quick meals at depot restaurants. Menus included greasy potatoes, buffalo steaks, elk, and antelope. But passengers didn't just see these wild Plains animals as meat on their plates. From their windows, riders saw buffalo and antelope herds crossing the grasslands. Sometimes men shot them through open windows.

Crossing the Plains by train was not always comfortable or safe. Tornadoes sometimes lifted a train right off the tracks. Winter blizzards half-buried entire trains in snow drifts. Once in a while, swarms of grasshoppers invaded the Plains and landed on the tracks in piles six inches deep. When the train ran over the insects, its wheels spun helplessly in the slime of crushed grasshopper bodies. The grasshopper problem led to the invention of the sand dome, a special container on the engine that poured sand onto the rails to give the wheels better grip.

Denver Public Library Western History Department

In the Nevada desert, a salty dust stung passengers' eyes and throats. Thunderstorms and floods washed out sections of track and caused ties and track to sink in mud. There were accidents too, due to bad construction. Some bridges collapsed under the weight of the first cross-country trains.

Pullman dining cars were elegant

Most riders, however, crossed to Utah without any problems. In Utah, passengers changed from Union Pacific to Central Pacific trains and continued on to Sacramento. About 150,000 people made the journey that first year of cross-country train travel.

FIRST COAST-TO-COAST TRAIN

The *Pullman Hotel Express* left Boston on May 23, 1870, bound for California. Merchants and members of wealthy Boston families boarded at the Boston & Albany station for the first transcontinental train trip that didn't require changing cars. The eight-car train had sleeping cars, hotel cars, a wine room, a barber shop, and two organs for entertainment. It also had its own newspaper, published and printed right on board. On arrival in San Francisco, a bottle of Atlantic Ocean water was mixed with water from the Pacific Ocean to symbolize the event.

Railroading Crews

The newly finished railroads created new jobs across the country. Each passenger and freight train had a team of workers called the running crew that kept it going. The engineer, fireman, brakemen, and conductor kept the wheels turning, the boilers stoked, and the train on track and on time—mostly.

The engineer had the important job of driving the train, but the conductor was the train boss. It was his job to make sure that everything ran smoothly. Conductors collected money for tickets, made sure passengers got off at the right stations, and sometimes removed passengers who became too rowdy.

When the conductor wanted the engineer to stop the train, he pulled a cord that was connected to a whistle in the engine cab. When the engineer heard the stop whistle, he signaled back with three blasts of his own whistle.

The engineer drove the locomotive from the right side of the cab. He controlled the speed of the train by opening or closing his throttle lever. To run at full speed, he kept his throttle wide open. This let the full force of steam push the pistons and rods that turned the driving wheels.

The engineer drove the train from the right side of the cab

"HOG-HEADS" AND "GREASEBALLS"

Railroaders had their own names for the jobs they did. Engineers were nicknamed "hog-heads" because they sometimes "hogged," or used too much, steam. The fireman was called "tallow-pot" because he always kept a potful of tallow-lard, which is hot animal fat, ready for greasing the engine. He was also called "greaseball," "smoke agent," and "water warmer." Conductors were called "skippers," "captains," and "brains" because they were in charge of the train.

The fireman loaded fuel into a fire-box

The engineer's assistant, called the fireman, usually rode on the left side of the cab. His main job was to keep the fire going in the boiler to make steam. He tossed wood or shoveled coal from the tender into a fire-box where the fuel was burned. The tender was an open-top car right behind the engine that was filled with a supply of wood or coal. Firemen were also responsible for shining the engine, filling the water tank, and greasing cylinders. If he did his job well, a fireman could one day become an engineer.

Brakemen had the most dangerous jobs on the train. When they heard the engineer's signal to stop, they ran across the top of the train, turning the brake wheels that stuck up at the end of each car. Stronger automatic air brakes weren't installed on most trains until the 1890s.

The brakeman's other risky job was to connect the train cars together, called coupling. To do this, he had to stand between two cars and hook them together with a link and pin. To uncouple the cars, the brakeman had to run alongside the moving train and quickly pull out the pin that connected the cars. Many brakemen were hurt when the heavy cars smashed their fingers, or even pulled them under the train.

A train's running crew also included a flagman or signalman who rode in the last car of the train, called the caboose. During the day he used different colored flags to signal to the engineer or other trains; at night he used a lantern. The caboose had a cook stove and bunks for the crew, and a special dome called a cupola built into the roof so the crew could look ahead to the engine.

The caboose had a dome on the roof called a cupola

Wrecks, Accidents, and Disasters

Pioneer railroading was a dangerous business. Steam engines were still a new invention, and until train crews learned the best way to run them, there were many accidents.

The first explosion of a locomotive occurred on June 17, 1831, in South Carolina. A fireman on the *Best Friend of Charleston* sat down on the boiler safety valve lever to quiet the rush of steam. He didn't know that letting steam escape was necessary to keep too much pressure from building up in the boiler. With no place for the steam to go, the boiler blew up. The fireman was thrown from the locomotive and three other crewmen were injured.

The men who built the transcontinental railroad thought more about finishing it quickly and cheaply than they did about safety. Often, bridges, tunnels, and roadbeds were poorly constructed. Train crews risked their lives on every trip. Problems with tracks also led to many accidents—ties rotted out, rails came loose, tracks sank in mud, drawbridges were left open, and trestles collapsed.

Early engineers often drove their engines too fast and were careless about safety. In Philadelphia, a train plowed into a horse and buggy at a grade crossing, where a road crossed the tracks. One rider in the buggy was killed and another injured. The engineer hadn't even slowed down.

In 1853, a New York & New Haven train plunged into a river, killing forty passengers and injuring eighty. The engineer hadn't noticed a "low-ball signal," which meant the drawbridge was open and the train should stop.

A 1913 train wreck

The Bettmann Archive

The Bettmann Archive

Only one car survived when this bridge collapsed

An engineer's mistake led to the fatal wreck of a circus train on June 22, 1918, in Indiana. The train had stopped on the tracks because of mechanical problems. A flagman stood behind the caboose to warn oncoming trains to stop. Suddenly, he saw the headlight of a train. He swung his signal lantern back and forth, but the oncoming train didn't slow down. The engineer had fallen asleep with his hand on the throttle! It plowed into the circus train, killing 68 people and the circus animals.

Train crews weren't always to blame. In the days before strict timetables, automatic signals, and telegraph messages, trains were often off schedule, and trains would sometimes be on the track at the wrong time. Train collisions were not uncommon.

To slow or stop a train, brakemen tightened handbrake wheels atop moving cars. They ran along narrow "cat-walks" on car roofs to get to the brakes. Sometimes they slipped on winter ice or were thrown from the train as it rocked. Brakemen also attached cars together with dangerous link and pin couplers. They had to stand between the cars and guide the link of one car into the socket of another. Many lost fingers, hands, or their lives in the process.

In 1872, George Westinghouse invented automatic air brakes. Then in 1873, Eli Janney invented automatic couplers. Both inventions reduced the risk of accidents to brakemen. But railroad companies wouldn't install the new systems until the 1890s when the government forced them to. They just didn't want to spend the money.

Brakemen were sometimes injured while coupling or uncoupling cars

Railroad safety has continued to improve during the last 100 years. But disasters still occur. In 1993, Amtrak's *Sunset Limited* plunged off a bridge into an alligator swamp in Alabama. Forty-seven people died. Earlier that night, a barge had crashed into the railroad bridge, making it too weak to support the train.

The Great Train Robberies

On the night of October 6, 1866, two masked men held up the Ohio & Mississippi Railway near Seymour, Indiana. The thieves simply walked through a passenger coach and into the unlocked express car. Express cars carried valuables, such as gold and silver from western mines and safes filled with payroll money. Express messengers rode with the valuables, but they didn't expect trouble.

The masked men surprised the messengers, held them at gunpoint, took $13,000 from the safe, then disappeared into the night. It was the first train robbery in U.S. history.

About a year later, the same train was held up again. Suspects were rounded up and one of them, John Reno, was sent to jail. But John wasn't the only robber in the Reno family. Four of his brothers later held up the Jefferson, Madison, & Indianapolis Railroad, killed a messenger, and got away with $96,000.

The Reno Gang had started a new profession—train robbery. By 1870, the Reno Gang had been captured and lynched —hanged without trial. But the age of train robberies was just beginning.

The first train robbery in the West happened around midnight on November 5, 1870. The Central Pacific's *Atlantic Express* left Oakland, California, carrying $41,800 in gold coins and $8,800 in silver. Some of the money was wages for workers at the Comstock mines in Nevada. In the Wells Fargo express car, agents were armed with rifles and sawed-off shotguns. As the train slowed down in heavy rain and fog near the town of Verdi, five masked men hopped aboard. Two entered the engine cab with guns pointed at the engineer and fireman. The other three uncoupled the cars behind the express car.

A robber single-handedly holds up an entire train

The Bettmann Archive

The outlaw Jesse James

While the engine, tender, and express cars continued up the track, the passenger coaches were left behind. Several miles outside of Verdi, the robbers told the engineer to stop the train. A sixth thief was waiting there with horses.

The express agents wondered why the train had stopped. They slid open the door and saw five shotguns pointed at them. With no time to reach for their weapons, they surrendered. The thieves, "Gentleman Jack" Davis and his "Knights of the Road," got away with $41,000 in gold coins.

The most famous U.S. outlaw, Jesse James, began his train robbing career on July 21, 1873. On that day he teamed up with his brother Frank and another family of brothers, the Youngers, to hold up the Rock Island line near Adair, Iowa. Along a sharp curve in the tracks, they loosened a rail and tied a rope to it. As the engine rounded the curve, the thieves yanked away the rail. The engine derailed, falling on its side and killing the engineer.

The thieves held guns on the train crew, emptied the express safe, and robbed the passengers. They escaped with $4,000. The James and Younger gangs continued to rob trains for the next eight years.

A DARING HOLDUP AND ESCAPE

A former cowboy named Oliver Perry was perhaps the most daring train robber of all time. On a freezing day in February 1891, he climbed atop the express car of a train near Syracuse, New York. Working alone, Perry lowered a rope ladder down one side of the car and climbed down. He slid open the unlocked door, swung in, and subdued the messenger. At the next stop, Perry jumped out with the money and made his getaway in a stolen locomotive.

Express safes contained gold, silver, and cash

Railroad Boom Towns

As cross-country track was laid across America from the east and the west, work trains followed the rails. They brought supplies and building materials to construction crews. The crews lived in temporary base camps set up at the end of the track where the rails ended. These camps were small tent towns, with housing for workers, construction headquarters, and supply stations.

After a few months, when new track was laid 100 or 200 miles farther up the line, the base camp packed up and moved by work train to the new end of track. In this way, base camps leap-frogged across the North American countryside.

A camp and construction train for Central Pacific crews

Base camps along Union Pacific track "boomed" overnight. Gold seekers, homesteaders, merchants, and adventurers followed the Union Pacific onto the Great Plains. So did gamblers and outlaws looking for easy money. They found it in the pockets of railroad workers.

North Platte, Nebraska, was the first railroad boom town on the Union Pacific line. About 2,000 laborers set up tents there in November 1866. Within a few weeks, North Platte had a main street lined with bars, dance halls, and gambling houses. Most of the businesses were set up in tents with false board fronts to make them look like real buildings.

TROUBLE IN PROMONTORY

Promontory, Utah, became the last rowdy railroad town when the Central and Union Pacific rail lines joined there in 1869. It was much like other railroad boom towns that had followed the Union Pacific line west. Tent saloons, gambling shacks, and cheap hotels lined a dirt street facing the railroad station. Liquor was in greater supply than water. And outlaws like Behind-the-Rock Johnny and gangs of gamblers like the Promontory Boys cheated travelers and railroaders.

North Platte and other railroad towns like it were called "Hell on Wheels" towns. Railroad workers stayed in one place for a few weeks, drinking, gambling, and fighting—and then suddenly packed up and left. Saloons and wild dance halls called hurdy-gurdy houses came down like stage sets and followed the railroad west.

After several months, North Platte picked up and moved to Julesburg, Colorado—the next base camp and boom town. Julesburg dance halls were quickly crowded with free-spending railroaders. Shootings and knifings occurred daily.

Workers drank liquor like it was water, spending their hard-earned pay on whiskies with names like Red Jacket, Blue Run, and Red Cloud. Two months later, almost the whole town of Julesburg moved down the line to Cheyenne, Wyoming. Canvas tents, saloons, and entire dance floors were transported by train.

Brawls were common in boom town saloons

The next stop was Benton in Wyoming's dry, hot desert. Thousands of railroaders, gold seekers, and swindlers found recreation at Benton's "Big Tent"—a combination saloon, dance hall, and gambling den. Two months later, Benton had disappeared. Its 23 saloons packed up overnight and moved on to Laramie.

Meanwhile, the Central Pacific was working its way east with Chinese construction crews. But "Hell on Wheels" towns didn't pop up along the Central Pacific line like they did on the Union Pacific. The Chinese workers didn't drink, and they gambled only with other Chinese.

Still, things weren't always quiet in the Central Pacific base camps. On May 6, 1869, bloody fighting broke out among Chinese crews at Camp Victory in Utah. One worker was killed in a battle fought with crowbars, spikes, and picks—all over a $15 gambling debt.

Workers take a break

Railroads Settle the West

After the Central Pacific and Union Pacific lines connected in Utah, the railroads were left with a problem. Their trains could now cross the country, but to make money the railroads needed to carry more passengers and freight. There were few towns and businesses on the Great Plains. The only freight traffic was on the Kansas Pacific line, which hauled cattle back East.

The railroads decided that the answer to their problem was to get more people to settle the Great Plains. The 1862 Homestead Act helped them achieve their goal. This Act promised 160 acres for just $18 to anyone who could farm the land for five years. Homesteaders by the thousands headed west for cheap land.

The Bettmann Archive

Homesteaders heading west

The government had granted free land along the tracks to the railroads as payment for building the railways. In all, the railroads received 130 million acres of free land. In the 1850s, the Illinois Central line sold one and a half million acres of this land to settlers moving west. During the 1870s, the Union Pacific and the Central Pacific lines began selling land to European immigrants and Americans moving west.

Railroad companies sent land agents to Europe and back East. Agents gave out brochures and guidebooks that described fertile farmland on America's Great Plains. The Union Pacific ran ads in 2,000 newspapers and magazines. The Northern Pacific advertised in German, Swiss, and Dutch newspapers. They also had more than 800 land agents in Great Britain and 100 more in Scandinavia and northern Europe.

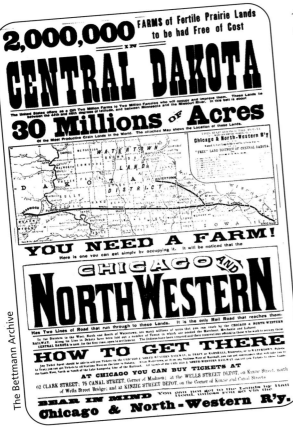

The Bettmann Archive

Railroad posters attracted settlers to western lands

Agents worked hard to attract immigrants who didn't have religious freedom or political rights in Europe. Posters pictured the Plains as a lush, green "Garden of Eden." Paintings showed fruits and vegetables covering the land. Desperate immigrants believed the agents and boarded ships bound for America, the "land of plenty."

In harbors and railway terminals back East, competition for settlers was fierce. Agents promised free land and farm equipment and packed people onto immigrant trains. But once the immigrants reached their land, they discovered that the western Plains didn't look much like the pictures in ads and posters.

Many farmers' crops failed on the dry Plains

Railroad companies had lied about farming conditions. They had claimed that "rain followed the plow," meaning that the dry Plains climate would change once farmers starting planting crops. In fact, drought was a constant threat on the wide grasslands.

Rain did fall for several years in the 1880s, but then stopped. Extreme heat caused crops to wither and die. There were other hardships as well. Homesteaders faced blizzards, lightning storms, prairie fires, dust storms, and grasshopper invasions.

About 2 million farms were created by railroad land sales. But many farms failed while the railroad companies thrived. Many homesteaders went broke, packed up, and left. Those who stayed adapted to the Plains. They irrigated, dug wells, and learned dry farming methods. By the early 1900s, Plains farmers were supplying grain to the world. The western railroads had succeeded in colonizing the Plains with farms.

IMMIGRANT CARS

To transport immigrants west, railroads provided special immigrant cars. These were little more than boxcars with double rows of narrow benches. Immigrants paid a special fare from New York to Omaha and another reduced fare from Omaha to their homesteads on the Plains. They were herded into the cars like cattle. Men, women, and children were packed ninety to a car and slept on the floor. By the time they arrived on the Plains, most families had spent most of their money on travel costs.

UPI/Bettmann

Immigrants traveled west in crowded trains

Tracks Cover the Nation

After the last spike was driven on America's first transcontinental line, other cross-country railroads followed. More than 100,000 miles of track were spiked and bolted down between 1870 and 1890. Railroads soon covered the nation, with 160,000 miles of track and five transcontinental systems. Every western town wanted a railroad running through it.

The Bettmann Archive

Several rail lines met at the depot in Durand, Michigan

During the 1870s, several railroad companies competed in building cross-country lines. The Texas & Pacific began building west across Texas to California in 1871. Meanwhile, the Southern Pacific line was building east from California to Texas. By 1877, the Southern Pacific track had reached the Arizona border. But the two companies disagreed about which line would build track across Arizona's desert.

While the government was deciding, the Southern Pacific secretly laid track in Arizona. The Texas & Pacific was angry with the Southern Pacific for breaking the rules, but it was too late. The tracks were already built, and the government sided with the Southern Pacific. By 1881, the Southern Pacific had crossed Arizona and New Mexico and reached El Paso, Texas. There the Southern Pacific and Texas & Pacific tracks were joined, creating a cross-country railroad across the southern U.S.

RAILROAD TIME

As railroad networks spanned the continent, time schedules became a problem. Eastern railroads had always run on local time, with the hour of day determined by the sun. But in California, 3,000 miles to the west, the sun set three hours later. Long distance travelers and railroaders were confused until 1883, when the country was divided into four time zones. All railroads within a zone ran on the same time. Clocks were adjusted as trains crossed into other zones.

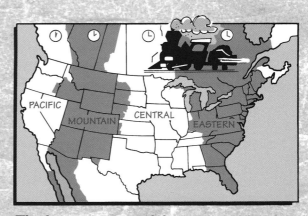

The four time zones of the continental U.S.

On the western Plains, other lines competed for cross-country routes. The Atchison, Topeka, & Santa Fe (A.T. & S.F.) built west across Kansas to Colorado. After reaching Colorado, the A.T. & S.F. turned south to enter New Mexico. At the same time, the Denver & Rio Grande railroad was building south from Denver through New Mexico to El Paso, Texas.

At the Raton Pass on the New Mexico border, the railroads fought over who would build through the pass. This valley was the best railroad route through the Rocky Mountains from Colorado to New Mexico. After several gun battles, the Santa Fe railroad won the route. But the railroads fought again over a route to the Colorado silver mines. Crews of both lines attacked each other with picks, shovels, and rifles. This time the Denver & Rio Grande line won.

The Santa Fe line continued building west across New Mexico and Arizona to the California border. There they were stopped by agents of the Southern Pacific and Texas & Pacific. The three railroads agreed on a deal that allowed the Santa Fe line to build across California to San Diego.

The New York Central soon had trains running on four tracks

The Northern Pacific railroad began work on a northern route around 1870. Crews built east from Puget Sound in Washington and west from Lake Superior in Minnesota. The route passed through the Yellowstone country of the Sioux nation. Native tribes fought the railroad, but couldn't stop the builders. On September 8, 1883, the last spike was driven, connecting 2,045 miles of Northern Pacific track.

A second northern route was completed ten years later. The Great Northern ran north of the Northern Pacific from Lake Superior to Spokane, Washington. By 1893, there were five cross-country rail routes in the U.S. This network of tracks brought an end to the wild frontier.

Farmers vs. the Railroad

Americans believed that the transcontinental railroad was built to benefit everyone. But Central and Union Pacific officials built it mainly to benefit themselves. For each mile of new track they built, the railroads received free land and government payments. Most of this money wound up in the pockets of railroad owners. By 1870 railroad owners were the most powerful men in the country.

During the 1870s, railroad companies in the West were getting even richer from the settlers who came west to farm. Homesteaders paid the railroad for land and also paid for train tickets to get there. Then they paid to have supplies sent out to their land, and paid again to ship their crops back East. Without the railroads, farmers couldn't make a living. Railroad owners took advantage of this.

UPI/Bettmann

Many homesteaders in Nebraska settled on land bought from the railroad

At the time, there were no laws limiting the price of fares and freight rates. Lawmakers and judges rode for free in exchange for supporting the railroads, but farmers and ordinary citizens had to pay the high rates the railroads charged.

Homesteaders suffered the most, because they were cheated twice by the railroad. First, the railroad's grain dealers paid the farmers too little for their crops, then the railroads charged them too much for transporting the grain to market. The profits went to the railroads, not to the farmers. Farmers were stranded on western lands with no choice but to pay, because nothing and no one got in or out except by railroad. Dishonest and powerful railroad men ruled the West like a kingdom.

The Bettmann Archive

Farmers at a Grange meeting

RAILROAD RIP-OFFS

In 1872 officials of the Union Pacific railroad were accused of bribing politicians so they would pass laws that supported the railroads. Bribing, which is illegal, means giving money to someone to make them do what you want. Congress looked into the matter and found that Vice President Schuyler Colfax had accepted $1,000 for his support of railroads. Congress also discovered that congressmen like James A. Garfield were actually part-owners of the Union Pacific. Garfield later became president of the United States. Politicians and railroad "barons" became rich and powerful even though the railroads they built later went broke.

Some railroad barons bribed politicians

Around 1874, farmers got together to fight the men they called the railroad "robber barons." The farmers started a group called the National Grange of the Patrons of Husbandry. They called their group the Grange, for short, and they called themselves Grangers. Husbandry and grange were old words for farming.

More than a million and a half Grangers agreed that farmers badly needed freight rates controlled. They believed that a democratic government had to protect its people from a few men who had all the power. Grangers began electing honest representatives to state governments. Soon states were passing laws and forming railroad commissions to control freight rates. In 1876, the Supreme Court decided that states had the right to control railroad dealings.

But the railroad barons fought back, and in 1886 the Supreme Court changed its decision in favor of the railroads. Then in 1887, Congress passed the Interstate Commerce Act to control railroad fares and freight rates. Railroading became the first private business to be controlled by the U.S. government.

The Bettmann Archive

After harvesting their crops, farmers sent them to market by rail

Railroaders, Hoboes, and Dreamers

Many different kinds of people were part of the development of the railroad in America. In a way, the railroad created its own society. At the top were rich investors in their San Francisco, New York, or Boston offices. At the bottom were the hoboes who rode the rails for free—when they didn't get caught. And in the middle were the trainmen—track builders and train crews. Together, they were the kings and queens of the Iron Horse and steel road.

From the start of rail travel, some people began sneaking aboard to ride without paying for a ticket. By the 1890s, there were about 60,000 wandering workers, tramps, and bums on U.S. railroads. The wandering workers called themselves "hoboes," or just "boes," from the French word *beau*, which means "fine" or "handsome." "Ho!" was a word of greeting. Hoboes rode on top, inside, under, and between train cars. Sometimes they "rode the blinds" the space between the baggage car and engine. They lived along the tracks in camps called "hobo jungles."

A woman called Boxcar Bertha hoboed on freight trains in the 1930s when many Americans were out of work. In her book, *Sister of the Road*, she wrote that a million and a half people were hoboing across the U.S. and Canada during the Great Depression of the 1930s. About 7,500 of them were women, according to Bertha. Some were out of work, some were criminals, and some were simply rebels.

One early king of the road was Charles H. Frisbie, born in 1822. When he was 15, Frisbie began work on a construction crew laying track for the Syracuse & Utica Railroad in New York. He drove a team of mules pulling construction supplies along wooden tracks. A year later, he was a fireman on the line's first locomotive.

By the late 1840s, Frisbie was an engineer on the Michigan Central. His engine derailed twice. Frisbie spent a year recovering from injuries—then went back to work. He ended his career as an engineer on the Burlington line.

UPI/Bettmann

Hobo Ernest Albright in 1938

During the Great Depression, more than a million hoboes—thousands of them women—rode the rails

Theodore "Crazy" Judah was a man with a dream. In the 1850s, he imagined a railroad across North America. Judah was a little ahead of his time, which is why people called him "Crazy." But he was right. His dream of a transcontinental railroad would become a reality.

Judah surveyed and mapped routes through California's mountains. When he needed money to begin building, he went to four rich California businessmen; together they were called the "Big Four." For Judah, it was a big mistake.

The businessmen wanted to build cheaply so they could make a bigger profit. Judah disagreed and decided to find less greedy investors. He boarded a ship for the East Coast, but became sick with yellow fever along the way. He died in New York. The Big Four were left to build Judah's dream, the Central Pacific. They took all the glory—and the profit.

HARVEY GIRLS

One drawback of train travel in the 1870s was the food. There were few dining cars, especially in the West. Travelers had to wolf down greasy meals in ten minutes at depot restaurants—until Fred Harvey came along. Harvey opened 47 restaurants in depots along the Santa Fe line that served good food in a comfortable setting. His waitresses were called Harvey Girls. They wore simple black and white uniforms and lived in dormitories. Harvey Girls earned $17.50 a month plus tips and room and board. About 5,000 Harvey Girls married railroaders.

Beginning in 1883, many young women headed west to become Harvey Girls

Legends, Songs, and Lingo

From the start, railroading inspired a language of its own. Slang expressions grew in number with railroad lines and the people who made them run. On the Atchison, Topeka, & Santa Fe, the expression "pinch her down" meant "reduce speed prior to stop." "Plug 'em" meant "use emergency brakes." "Siftin' through the dew" was "traveling at high speed."

Railroad workers brought different skills, histories, and cultures to their work. Irish immigrants brought folk ballads. Freed slaves brought old African rhythms and vocal harmonies.

Crews called section gangs worked at straightening and repairing track. The song "Can'cha Line 'Em" was sung by section gangs in Louisiana. A foreman directed the gang to a section of crooked track, shouting:

The Bettmann Archive

Union Pacific workers

> *All right, now, run down to the second joint ahead,*
> *And touch it easy! Quick! I hear the train coming!*

After the gang jammed their heavy crowbars under the rail, a song leader sang out:

> *All I hate about lining track,*
> *These old bars about to break my back!*

The gang then heaved against the rail, singing:

> *Ho, boys, can'cha line 'em?...*
> *See as we go lining track!*

Railroad work songs took on the rhythm of the work being done. "Drillers" swung heavy hammers down on steel drills, driving holes for blasting powder. A "turner" held the drill in place as two drillers hammered it down. As he swung his hammer, the driller sang a phrase, then brought his hammer down on the drill. With each hammer blow, the steel rang out:

> *This old hammer, (ring!) Rings like silver, (ring!)*
> *Shines like gold, (ring!) Shines like gold. (ring!)*

The most famous steel driver of all time was John Henry. He drilled for the Chesapeake & Ohio (C & O) Railroad around 1873. At that time, the C & O was blasting out the Big Bend Tunnel in West Virginia. John Henry was the most powerful driller on the crew. The railroad decided to match its new steam-powered drill in a contest against John Henry. The folk ballad "John Henry" tells the story in song:

CASEY JONES, A BRAVE ENGINEER

The legend of Casey Jones is based on fact. John Luther "Casey" Jones was born near the town of Cayce, Kentucky, and became an engineer on the Illinois Central around 1900. He had a reputation as a daredevil. On the night of April 26, 1906, he was driving engine No. 638 on the Cannonball Express when he saw a boxcar sitting on his track up ahead. Casey tried to stop, but there wasn't time. He died with one hand on his whistle cord and the other on his brake—too brave to jump before wrecking.

The Bettmann Archive

Casey Jones

John Henry told his captain,
"A man ain't nothing but a man,
And before I'd let that steam-drill beat me down,
I'd die with this hammer in my hand."

In the song, John Henry drilled faster than the steam-drill and died doing it. In real life, he survived and continued to drill the Big Bend Tunnel, until he was crushed in a cave-in.

Railroads inspired more than work songs. Across the U.S., people heard the lonesome whistle and felt the pounding wheels of railroad trains. Sounds of steam locomotives and diesel engines found their way into North American folk and pop music. Country fiddlers played tunes like "The Orange Blossom Special," and jazz musicians played "The Chattanooga Choo-Choo." Today, blues and rock musicians sometimes make the sound of "high-balling"—fast-moving trains—with steel guitars.

John Henry was the most famous steel driver of all time

In Their Own Words

Old-time railroaders, passengers, and newspaper reporters gave first-hand accounts of the early days of railroading. Reading their words is the next best thing to being there.

J. O. Wilder worked on the Central Pacific and Southern Pacific lines for 54 years. His first job was as a back flagman on the Central Pacific survey crew. Back flagmen held flagpoles to help surveyors map straight routes over long distances. Wilder retired from railroad work in 1920, but remembered his early years:

On May 30, 1866, I left my home in San Francisco, a mere youth of 16, with my blankets and carpet sack, canvas pants, high-top boots, and seven and a half dollars in my pockets . . . to take my place in the employ of the Central Pacific Railroad. . . .

After breakfast the first morning, I was shown how to hold the red and white rod with sharp point on one end. . . . My hands were soft and I was soon changing from one to the other and had blisters on both.

On November 9, 1868, a California newspaper described the scene of Central Pacific Railroad construction in Utah:

Foremen are galloping here and there on horseback giving or receiving orders. Swarms of laborers, Chinese, Europeans, and Americans are hurrying to their work. On one side of the track stands the moveable blacksmith shop where a score of smiths are repairing tools and shoeing horses and mules.

MEMORIES OF A "NEWS BUTCHER"

Boys as young as ten or 12 years old worked on railroad trains selling newspapers, candy, drinks, and books. They were called "train boys," "newsboys," and "news butchers." Ernest Haycox was a news butcher working the rail line from Oakland to Sacramento, California. He describes his selling style:

Right after we pulled out, I started . . . by going through the train with salted peanuts. . . . The old-time butchers had taught me—first, get everybody in the train thirsty, then break out the soda pop and ice cream.

The Bettmann Archive

A newsboy selling books

Workers digging a train out of a snowdrift in Utah

In Great Plains blizzards, huge snowbanks drifted over the tracks. Train crews would uncouple the engine, back it up, and ram it through the banks. They called this "bucking the snow." Sometimes two or more engines were coupled together for more power. Cy Warman of the Kansas Pacific plowed double engines through 18-foot drifts one winter. He described how it looked:

> *Often when we came to a stop only the top of the stack of the front engine would be visible. . . . All this time the snow kept coming down, day and night, until the only signs of a railroad across the range were the tops of the telegraph poles.*

In 1829, a young engineer named Horatio Allen was the first to drive a steam locomotive in the U.S. Few believed that Allen would survive the test. Here's how he described his journey:

> *The impression was . . . that the iron monster would either break down the road or . . . leave the track at the curve and plunge into the creek. . . . My reply to such apprehension was . . . that I would take the first ride alone. . . . As I placed my hand on the throttle-valve handle I was undecided whether I would move slowly or with . . . speed. But believing that the road would be safe . . . I started with considerable velocity, passed the curve over the creek, and was soon out of hearing of the cheers. . . . At the end of two or three miles, I reversed the valves and returned . . . having thus made the first railroad trip by locomotive in the Western Hemisphere.*

In 1829, Horatio Allen drove the first locomotive in the U.S.

Railroads and the Environment

Railroads played a major role in settling the Great Plains. In the 1860s, the Kansas Pacific established depots in western Kansas for shipping cattle to markets back East. In the 1870s, railroads sold land to homesteaders and transported them onto the Plains. By settling the Plains with farms and cattle ranches, railroads helped close the American frontier. But what was America's last frontier like before the railroad?

The Great Plains ecosystem was a living environment of grasslands, river valleys, animals, and native peoples. Wild grasses swept the Plains from the Missouri River to the Rocky Mountains and from Texas to Canada. These native grasses provided a protective layer of sod that held the land together like a skin.

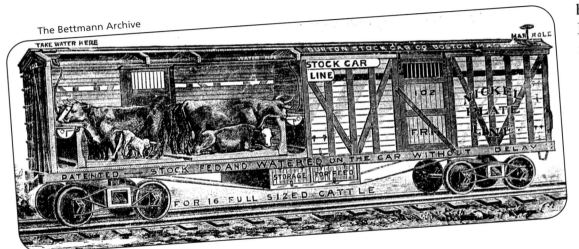

The Bettmann Archive

Stock cars transported cattle by rail

Great herds of buffalo roamed the Plains feeding on native bunch grasses. Cheyenne, Sioux, and other Plains Indians hunted buffalo and elk for food, clothing, and shelter. The Indians took only what they needed from the land, leaving the grasslands and river valleys mostly undisturbed.

The Iron Horse disrupted this balance of people and nature. Beginning in 1868, Texas cowboys drove herds of longhorn cattle across the Plains to railroad stops in Kansas. Cattletowns like Abilene were depots for shipping cattle to Chicago slaughterhouses. Native tribes and the buffalo were driven out of the Plains or killed. In their place, 8 million cows covered the prairie.

Each beef cow on the long drive ate 900 pounds of grass and shrubs in a month. Their powerful hooves beat the ground bare of native plants. Overgrazing destroyed the sod. Over time, lush grasslands became deserts.

Homesteading farmers also changed the Plains. Homesteaders plowed the dry grasslands, planted wheat and corn, and waited for rain. During many years, no rain came. Farmers struggled through the dry years by digging wells, irrigating, and planting crops that could survive without much water. Wild oats and bluegrass replaced native buffalo grasses and brought new plant diseases to the Plains that killed off more native vegetation.

THE IRON HORSE AND THE BUFFALO

For Plains Indians, buffalo were the source of life. But the railroad quickly changed the native way of life on the Plains. In order to drive native tribes from the path of the Iron Horse, the railroaders attacked their food supply—the buffalo. Hunters with high-powered rifles were hired to slaughter buffalo by the thousands. Men were encouraged to shoot them from moving trains. By 1887, fewer than 1,000 buffalo remained of the native herds of millions.

The Bettmann Archive

Some passengers shot buffalo from moving trains

In the early 1900s, rainfall came to the Plains. Wheat fields thrived during this wet cycle. Homesteaders rushed to plow up more land for fields, tearing up the Plains' protective skin. Then drought struck again in 1931. Without grass to anchor it, topsoil dried to dust and was picked up by windstorms. Dust storms filled the sky, blocking the sun. Parts of the southern Great Plains became known as the "Dust Bowl."

When the dust finally cleared, Plains farmers changed their farming methods. Instead of clearing as much land as they could for planting all at once, farmers started to rotate their crops. Rotating meant that farmers planted on certain fields during one year, then gave those fields a rest the next year. This allowed the soil to stay healthier.

After World War II (1939-1945), Plains farmers began using chemicals on their crops to kill insect pests and to make their plants grow bigger. But many of these chemicals left dangerous poisons in the water, air, and soil. Farmers of today continue to search for farming methods that yield large crops without damaging the environment.

The Bettmann Archive

An abandoned farm in Oklahoma during the Dust Bowl

Railroads Past, Present, and Future

American railroads continued to change and develop through the late 1800s. Between 1880 and 1890, railroad companies built 65,000 miles of new track. Single track railroads expanded to double track, triple track, and more. In the Northeast states, four-track and six-track lines were built to handle more passenger and freight traffic.

Huge terminals were built in major cities. Chicago became the junction, or railroad transfer point, between East and West. Until the late 1940s, every traveler and every suitcase switched trains at Chicago terminals.

During the 1890s and 1900s, small railroad companies combined with larger ones. The Pennsylvania Railroad system expanded to include 700 smaller lines. The New York Central grew to include 600 lines. These mergers had one goal in mind—profit.

The old-time railroad barons were retiring around this time, but the men who replaced them were just as greedy. Instead of spending money to improve their tracks and cars, they invested in other businesses. The owners grew wealthy as American railroads decayed. Trains and tracks were in poor condition by 1914, when World War I began.

Trains were desperately needed for wartime transportation. Troops and supplies had to be moved quickly to port cities for shipment overseas to Europe. But tracks, roadbeds, and bridges across the country all needed to be repaired. To get the job done, the U.S. government took temporary control of the nation's railroads.

Three locomotives—a gas turbine (left), a steam engine (middle), and a diesel-electric—lined up at Green River, Wyoming

The Bettmann Archive

Throughout the history of railroading, new inventions and materials improved railways despite their greedy owners. Worn iron rails were replaced with longer, stronger, and heavier steel rails. Cross-ties were also improved. Around 1875, wood ties were treated with preservative oils to keep them from rotting. Better rails and ties reduced the need for track repair.

Union Station, Chicago

Locomotives improved too. The American-style steam engine was used through the 1850s and 1860s. These locomotives had four leading wheels and four driving wheels. The leading wheels, called the "truck," guided the locomotives around tight curves. In 1863 the extra-powerful *Mogul* engine, with a two-wheel truck and six driving wheels, was pounding the rails. Engines were painted in bright colors until the 1870s, when the standard color became basic black. Railroad baron Commodore Vanderbilt came up with the idea to save money.

By the 1890s, passenger trains traveled at about 60 miles an hour. In 1893, the New York Central engine No. 999 set a 100-mile-an-hour record. Then in 1905, the Pennsylvania Railroad's *Broadway Limited* broke all records when it hit 127 miles an hour. But the steam engine's days were numbered. Electric and diesel fuel engines would soon take their place.

FLOATING TRAINS

Railroads of the future are already operating in England and Germany. Unlike their forerunners, these high-speed trains don't run on wheels or tracks. They float, or levitate, over a magnetic guideway. The magnetic levitation train—or maglev, for short—can reach speeds up to 300 miles per hour. Electricity flows through magnets under the train to create magnetic force. This force lifts the train and powers it along the guideway. Maglev travel is cleaner and quicker than diesel.

A Japanese maglev train

The first train powered by electricity ran on the Nantasket Branch of the New York, New Haven, & Hartford line in 1895. The B & O first used electric trains in its Baltimore tunnel. By 1914, the New Haven Railroad had completely electrified its line between New York and New Haven. Electricity worked best on the shorter lines running between cities and suburbs. The electric engines didn't clog tunnels with smoke the way steam engines did.

On the western plains, railroads continued to use steam engines into the 1930s. But in 1934, the Burlington line tested its new diesel-electric *Zephyr* engine. It used oil fuel to power the engine's electric generators. The generators in turn transferred power to the engine's driving wheels.

WWII soldiers sleeping on a troop train

Diesels were first used for hauling freight on the Santa Fe line in 1941. They were cheaper to run and needed less upkeep than steam locomotives. The sleek 5,000-horsepower diesels were built of stainless steel, aluminum, and other metals. Almost all of the 21,000 locomotives operating in the U.S. today are diesel-electric.

During World War II, American railroads transported nearly all troops and military freight. After the war, improved technologies were applied to railroading. Dispatchers used central control boards to check on the location of trains, set signals, and move trains to other tracks by remote control. Radio signals sent messages to train crews. But fewer people were riding the trains. A new age of automobile and airplane travel had begun.

After the 1940s, railroads again fell into disrepair. By 1970, bankrupt passenger lines were taken over by the U.S. government's Amtrak system. In 1976, the government saved Northeastern passenger lines by forming Conrail. Freight lines survived in better shape. Each day, some 10,000 freight trains haul goods across the country. Central computer systems control train traffic.

Today, the United States still has the largest rail system in the world, with 167,964 miles of track. The Iron Horse rides on.

INDEX